CW00933263

Crannogs
Lake-dwellings of early Ireland

Aidan O'Sullivan

Country House, Dublin

First published in 2000 by
Town House and Country House Ltd,
Trinity House, Charleston Rd
Ranelagh, Dublin 6
ISBN: 1-86059-091-8

© Aidan O'Sullivan 2000
All rights reserved. No part of this publication may be copied,
reproduced, stored in a retrieval system, broadcast or transmitted in any
form or by any means, electronic, mechanical, photocopying, recording
or otherwise without prior permission in writing from the publishers.
A CIP catalogue record for this book is available from the British Library.

Series editor: Dr Michael Ryan
Printed in Spain by Estudios Graficos ZURE

CONTENTS

WHAT ARE CRANNOGS?

Crannogs can be defined as wholly or largely artificial circular or oval islands in lakes. They were usually built of dumped layers of peat, brushwood, heavier timbers, stone and soil, and many were originally surrounded by a palisade or fence of closely-set vertical timber and roundwood posts.

Crannogs are among the most evocative and intriguing archaeological sites found in the Irish landscape. The quiet, abandoned appearance of crannogs as they survive today – as small, tree-clad islands in lakes or as stone cairns and earthen mounds around lake-shores – bears little resemblance to what observers a thousand years ago would have seen, when many crannogs were busy, prosperous lake dwellings.

Irish archaeologists have barely begun to explore the many functions that they served. Some may have been defended farmsteads, where men, women and children could have lived and worked in safety. We also know that many crannogs were royal residences, where kings, surrounded by their retinue of stewards, warriors, craftsmen, labourers and slaves, would have resided at certain times of the year, for feasting and carousing or for negotiating political settlements. Other crannogs may have been used only as places for metalworkers or other craftsmen to practise their trades. It is also possible that some crannogs were used by local communities as refuges from raiding armies, or as places to store valuable objects.

Studying crannogs

Crannogs are particularly important to archaeologists because their waterlogged condition means that rich, complex archaeological deposits are often preserved. Modern scientific archaeological excavation techniques can reveal abundant evidence for wooden houses, palisades and pathways, as well as thousands of metal, glass, wooden, bone and leather artefacts buried in their domestic and industrial rubbish. Because crannogs are usually waterlogged, ancient plant remains, seeds, beetles, animal bone and other clues to past economies and living conditions are also there to be discovered.

Fig. 1: Reconstruction drawing of a typical Irish north midlands crannog, constructed of a stone cairn with an oak palisade and an outer, defensive post palisade. The site is approached by a zigzagging causeway. There have been various attempts to reconstruct the appearance of an early Irish crannog, but it is likely that they varied widely in form and character. (Aidan O'Sullivan)

5

Fig. 2: The earliest reconstruction drawing of an Irish crannog, published in 1886 as the frontispiece of William G. Wood-Martin's masterful synthesis, The Lake Dwellings of Ireland. This drawing, done by William Wakeman, has had a major influence down through the years on the way people imagine these sites to have looked.

Fig. 2: The earliest reconstruction drawing of an Irish crannog, published in 1886 as the frontispiece of William G. Wood-Martin's masterful synthesis, The Lake Dwellings of Ireland. *This drawing, done by William Wakeman, has had a major influence down through the years on the way people imagine these sites to have looked.*

Undoubtedly the golden age of crannog scholarship was during the late nineteenth century, when Irish antiquarians busily described, sketched and dug into crannogs all around the country. Many crannogs were discovered during the large-scale arterial drainage works and wetland reclamation projects then going on in Ireland's lakeland regions. As lake levels were lowered, many small islands and cairns emerged from the water and these were found to have evidence for ancient settlement.

For example, between 1839 and 1848, Sir William Wilde recorded the exciting archaeological discoveries being made by local labourers on the crannog of Lagore, near Dunshaughlin, County Meath. Other scholars of this time, such as William Wakeman and George Kinahan, were particularly active, and ventured further afield into the Irish landscape where they systematically surveyed and described these crannogs and lake-dwellings.

This scholarly interest in lake-dwellings was a Europe-wide phenomenon. Swiss, German and Scottish antiquarians of the time were also excited by the rich archaeological deposits being found in their own countries' lake villages and island dwellings. By 1886, Irish antiquarians had discovered at least 220 crannogs. In that year, the Sligo landlord William Gregory Wood-Martin published a major book

Fig. 3: William Wilde, one of the earliest crannog researchers in Ireland. Wilde made a visit in 1839 to Lagore, near Dunshaughlin, Co. Meath, when local labourers' diggings for bone for fertiliser first exposed the seventh to tenth century 'royal' crannog of the Early Medieval kings of southern Brega. (Rhoda Kavanagh)

entitled *The Lake Dwellings of Ireland or ancient lacustrine habitations of Erin commonly called crannogs.*

For several decades afterwards, fewer Irish antiquarians continued crannog research, but then a major leap forward came in the 1930s, when the American-funded Harvard Archaeological Expedition came to Ireland and excavated three major sites: the crannogs known to archaeologists as Ballinderry crannogs No. 1 and No. 2 (the first of which is in County Westmeath and the second in County Offaly), and Lagore crannog in County Meath.

These excavations had a major impact on Irish archaeology generally, as they demonstrated the importance of scientific excavation techniques and they produced very large collections of finds, many of which continue to influence the interests of Irish archaeologists. In recent years, Irish crannog research has been thriving in various ways, through a combination of archaeological survey and excavation and underwater investigations.

Even after 160 years of study (since Lagore crannog was first visited by William Wilde in 1839), however, Irish archaeologists remain puzzled and intrigued by many

Fig. 4: William Wakeman, an indefatigable recorder during the 1870s of crannogs in the north-west of Ireland, where he took careful note of their structures and finds. Wakeman was to provide most of the illustrations for Wood-Martin's Lake Dwellings of Ireland. (Journal of the Royal Society of Antiquaries of Ireland)

Fig. 5: William
Wakeman's general
view, plan and
cross-section of a
crannog on
Ballydoolough,
Co. Fermanagh.
These remarkable
drawings provide
useful information
on the appearance
of many of these
sites when they
were first exposed
in the 19th century.
(Wood-Martin's
Lake Dwellings
of Ireland)

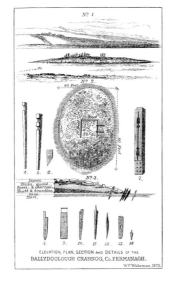

Fig. 5: William
Wakeman's general
view, plan and
cross-section of a
crannog on
Ballydoolough,
Co. Fermanagh.
These remarkable
drawings provide
useful information
on the appearance
of many of these
sites when they
were first exposed
in the 19th century.
(Wood-Martin's
Lake Dwellings
of Ireland)

Fig. 6: Dug-out
boat lying beside
the wooden
palisade of the
Early Medieval
site of Ballinderry
crannog No. 2,
Co.Offaly. This
crannog was one
of three excavated
by the Harvard
Archaeological
Expedition to
Ireland in the
1930s, excavations
which continue to
shape our
understanding
of these lake-
dwellings.
(Proceedings
of the Royal Irish
Academy)

aspects of the archaeology of crannogs and
lake-dwellings. Perhaps after all this time we
have only started properly to explore the
archaeology of these enigmatic sites, so that
many discoveries and surprises await us in the
years ahead.

Crannogs through the centuries

The origins and chronology of Irish crannogs
are still not very well understood, but we do
know that people have been living by Ireland's
lake-shores since earliest times. There is good
evidence for lake-shore settlements in the
Mesolithic (7000–4000 BC) and Neolithic
(4000–2500 BC) periods and in the Bronze Age
(2500–600 BC). However, crannogs as we know them were only built from the Early
Medieval (AD 500–1200) period onwards, beginning in the late sixth and early
seventh centuries AD, as has been shown by scientific tree-ring dating of timbers
from crannogs in Antrim, Fermanagh and Down.

We do not know why people began to build crannogs and other lake-dwellings,
but we can surmise that it was due to a combination of political instability, climatic
deterioration and population increase which made it necessary for an anxious people

to defend their kin and property on isolated islands.

Crannogs were being built in Scotland at a slightly earlier period, in the third to fifth centuries AD, and it has been suggested that the idea of building and living on artificial defended islets was first introduced into Ireland by means of the strong contacts between the people of north-east Ireland and south-west Scotland. Perhaps crannogs were built just because it was the fashion, as wealthy farmers, lords and kings became interested in acquiring the status and prestige that would have accrued to the owner of such a highly visible and difficult-to-construct island settlement.

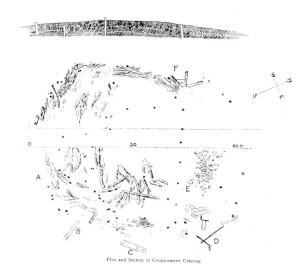

Plan and Section of Craigywarren Crannog.

Fig. 7: Plan of a small Early Medieval crannog excavated at Craigywarren, Co. Antrim. It is possible that this site, unlike many others, was abandoned not long after its construction. (Proceedings of the Royal Irish Academy)

Once built, crannogs could have been occupied for widely varying periods - for weeks, months, or centuries. Indeed, some crannogs may only have been lodges for use in the warm, dry months of summer, while others may have been permanent residences for people who chose to stay out on the island all year. Some crannogs appear to have been built, lived on and then abandoned very quickly. Craigywarren crannog in County Antrim and Bofeenaun crannog in County Mayo are both small sites that appear to have had single-phase occupations, used for perhaps only ten to fifteen years. In contrast, other sites were occupied for at least several generations. Ballinderry crannog No. 1 was occupied for much of the seventh century, while Ballinderry crannog No. 2 had two phases of use in the late tenth and early eleventh centuries AD.

There is also good archaeological and historical evidence which suggests that several Irish crannogs witnessed very long periods of use and reconstruction before their final destruction or abandonment. Moynagh Lough was inhabited for at least two hundred years (in the seventh and eighth centuries AD), while Lagore crannog was probably occupied for an even longer period (from the sixth to the eleventh century AD).

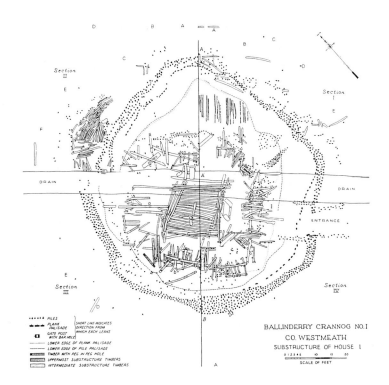

BALLINDERRY CRANNOG NO.I
CO. WESTMEATH
SUBSTRUCTURE OF HOUSE 1
SCALE OF FEET

Most crannogs were occupied in the Early Medieval period (AD 500–1200), a period of profound internal social and economic change in Ireland, and there may well have been significant differences in the function and role of crannogs at different times. Perhaps the earliest crannogs in the sixth and seventh centuries were mostly small, defended homesteads, enclosed within small, lightly built wooden palisades, which may have been the residences of local lords or wealthy farmers and craftsmen. In the eighth century, however, some crannogs could have evolved into centres of greater social and political importance, being gradually enlarged and enclosed within larger timber palisades and attracting itinerant metalworkers.

There is certainly evidence for what we might call 'mega-crannogs' (such as Lagore, Moynagh Lough, Ardakillen, Rathtinaun) by the ninth and tenth centuries. These were probably the large, well-defended lake-dwellings of regionally powerful kings, which were inhabited by a socially diverse, wealthy community with far-flung trading contacts throughout Ireland and north-western Europe.

There is also good archaeological and historical evidence that crannogs were used throughout the Late Medieval (1200–1534) and Early Modern (1534–1650) periods, when they served as lordly residences, as defended strongholds in times of danger, as storehouses for ammunition, gold and silver and as prisons and hospitals. Indeed the Irish word *crannóg*, meaning a small island built with young trees, is only used in the native Irish annals from the thirteenth century onwards. From this time on, the destruction of crannogs during storms, high winds and military raids is frequently mentioned in the annals. There is also tree-ring dating evidence, from sites in Fermanagh, that oak palisades were being built on crannogs in the late fifteenth and early sixteenth centuries.

During the Tudor re-conquest of Ireland (1555–1603), it is clear that the destruction of Gaelic Irish crannogs was considered a vital task by English forces, who recognised them as hot-spots of rebellion and resistance and used cannon, fire and troops in often costly battles against their defenders. Even after this phase of destruction and the waning of the Gaelic Irish social order, many crannogs remained in use as fishing platforms, vegetable gardens or as refuges for vagabonds into the eighteenth century. Indeed, some crannogs are still used by duck-shooters and fishermen today.

Where crannogs are found

The archaeological surveys being carried out by the National Monuments Service in the Republic and by the Environment and Heritage Service in Northern Ireland show that there are at least 1200 known crannogs on the island of Ireland. However, hundreds, if not thousands, of other crannogs and lake-dwellings probably remain to be recorded in Ireland's lakeland regions, undiscovered because they are submerged under water, hidden under marshy vegetation or buried in waterlogged clays and peats.

Crannogs and lake-dwellings are, by definition, typically found only in those regions of Ireland abounding in lakes and fens: the midlands, west and north-west. Crannogs are particularly concentrated in the lakelands of the drumlin belt, which runs across counties Monaghan, Cavan, Leitrim and Fermanagh. There are lesser numbers of crannogs in the south midlands, east and north-east, although as it happens this is where Irish archaeologists have traditionally concentrated their research.

11

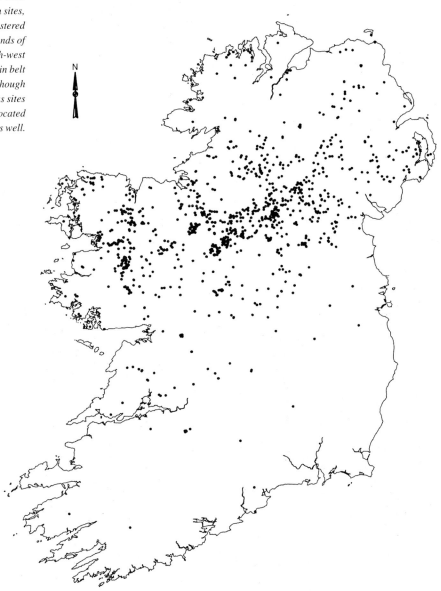

Fig. 9:
Distribution map
of crannogs in
Ireland. There are
at least 1200
known sites,
mostly clustered
in the lakelands of
the north-west
and drumlin belt
regions, although
numerous sites
are located
elsewhere as well.

Crannogs tend to be found in smaller lakes, possibly because the exposed shores of very large lakes like Lough Ree, Lough Derg or Lough Erne were too windswept and stormy.

Crannogs were sometimes built in shallow water along the lake-edge, where natural shoals and slight rises would have served as a useful foundation. Occasionally they can be found out in deeper water, maybe hundreds of metres out from the lake-shore, where much more labour and effort would have been needed to raise a mound of wood and stone. Crannog builders would have had to make a choice between isolation and ease of access according to local social and political circumstances.

Irish and Scottish crannogs, like ringforts and stone forts, were generally a dispersed form of rural settlement. This contrasts with the prehistoric and Early Medieval lake villages and defended fortresses of central and eastern Europe, where large communities lived together in villages on the lake-shore. Nevertheless, we can envisage an occasional loosely connected community of Irish lake-shore dwellers, as crannogs can be found in small groups or as sites located at regular intervals along lake shores. However, we do not know whether such groups of crannogs were all

Fig. 10: Aerial photograph of a crannog known as Goose Island (occupied in the ninth and tenth centuries AD), on the eastern shores of Lough Ennell, Co. Westmeath. A view of the crannog was incorporated into the vista of the lake provided by landscape gardening for the 18th century demesne of Belvedere, on the lakeshore. (Cambridge University Committee for Aerial Photography: AVH–13)

13

built and inhabited at around the same time, or whether they were built as a sequence of sites over time. Also, crannogs were merely the wetland settlements of wider local and regional territories; other people would also have been living within sight of these islands on the neighbouring drylands.

How crannogs were built

Of the 1200 known crannogs in Ireland, our knowledge of the construction techniques used to build them is mostly based on the evidence from the eight or nine

Fig. 11: Aerial photograph of O'Boyle's Fort on Loughadoon, Co. Donegal, a stone cashel on a natural island. Crannogs were not the only form of lake-dwelling used in Early Medieval Ireland; many island stone forts and also monastic islands are known to have been used. (Cambridge University Committee for Aerial Photography: ALQ–81)

14

sites that have been excavated to modern standards. Most of these excavated crannogs are in the north-east, midlands and east of the island, where timber, brushwood and peat were the main local building material. In other regions or localities, surveys indicate that crannogs were predominantly built of mounds of boulders and stones, occasionally using vertical wooden posts. Many of these boulder mounds retain little evidence for wooden structures, although these could have been eroded and washed away over the centuries leaving only the rubble behind.

Crannogs vary widely in size: some are mere islets measuring about 10–15 metres in diameter (for example Craigywarren and Ballinderry crannog No. 1), while much larger crannogs are also known (such as Moynagh Lough, Ballinderry crannog No. 2 and Lagore), often enclosing an internal circular or oval space measuring 30–40 metres across This range in size may be related to the wealth and needs of their inhabitants, the length of time the crannogs were occupied or the particular function they played in the settlement landscape. Sometimes a small islet (5–8m diameter) can be found right beside a much larger crannog. Perhaps the larger islands were domestic settlements and their neighbouring islets were used only as fishing platforms or as safe places for iron-working and other processes requiring the use of furnaces.

Building a crannog must have been a laborious, even a dangerous, task, requiring many weeks or months of work to gather together the raw materials and then put them in place. A large team of labourers working from dug-out boats or rafts could have first laid a substantial foundation of planks and cleft timber beams on the lake-bed, anchoring or retaining them in place with vertical wooden piling. The crannog

Fig. 12: A remarkable cross-section drawing of a crannog at Ardakillen, Co. Roscommon. Some of the best records of Irish crannogs made in the 19th century were these drawings and elevations done by engineers during land drainage schemes in the north-west. This standard of recording was certainly not practised by many contemporary antiquarians. (Wood-Martin's Lake Dwellings of Ireland 1886)

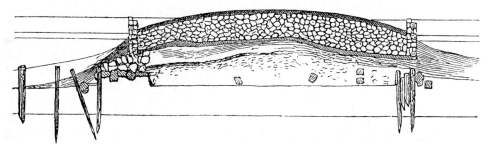

Fig. 152.

*Fig. 13: Plan
of a very large
circular wooden
house excavated
by John Bradley
at Moynagh
Lough crannog,
Co. Meath. This
structure
measured over
11m in diameter
and had a double
post wall, two
hearths and
sleeping areas
marked out with
posts. It was
almost certainly a
'royal' dwelling.
(Journal of the
Royal Society of
Antiquaries
of Ireland)*

was then built up by depositing successive layers of peat, heather, brushwood, timber and stone onto the slowly rising surface of the mound. The sides of the crannog cairn or mound would have been retained by a wooden revetment or palisade driven down into the lakebed around the site. Some crannogs, such as Ardakillen in County Roscommon and Lough Faughaun in County Down, appear to have been enclosed within low stone walls, perhaps built during their medieval phases of occupation.

Houses on crannogs

We know very little about the type of wooden structures that were built on Irish crannogs. Indeed, some crannogs such as the recently excavated crannogs at Bofeenaun, County Mayo have little or no evidence for houses. Many crannogs may not have been dwelling places at all, but merely artificial mounds to mark territorial boundaries or routeways.

It is true that houses have been clearly identified in a few of the excavated crannogs, such as Ballinderry crannog No. 1 and Moynagh Lough. At Moynagh Lough, a multi-period crannog has been excavated, on which there were at least three large, circular wooden houses in the seventh and eighth centuries AD. Significantly, one of these houses was exceptionally large, measuring at least 11m in diameter. This was obviously an important dwelling (a king's feasting house, perhaps), with a double post-and-wattle wall, two stone-lined hearths and rows of posts which divided it up into separate sleeping areas.

Contd. p.33

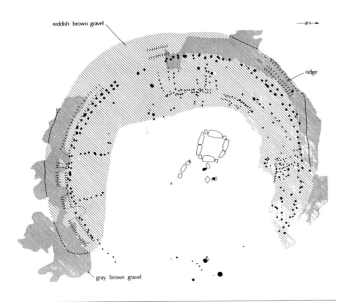

reddish brown gravel

ridge

gray brown gravel

Pl 1: A cairn of stone covered in trees is all that appears on the surface today of this crannog on Lough Meelagh, Co. Roscommon. Buried within this cairn there is probably well-preserved evidence of both its Early Medieval and Late Medieval occupation (Aidan O'Sullivan)

Pl 2: Archaeologists returning from their inspection of a crannog on Lough Gara, Co. Sligo in 1952. Many prehistoric lake-dwellings and Early Medieval crannogs were revealed when the waters dropped after drainage schemes on this lake at the time. (Dept. of Archaeology, NUI Galway)

17

CRANNOGS

Pl 3: A crannog cairn with its causeway lies exposed in shallow water near the shore at Annagose, Co. Monaghan. Not all of these lake-dwellings were constructed in inaccessible locations, and proximity to good agricultural land, for gardening and cattle pasture, would have been an important influence on their siting. (Dúchas – the Heritage Service)

Pl 4: Aerial photograph of a possible crannog on Lough-na-cranagh, Fair Head, Co. Antrim. This island is enclosed within a stone wall of unknown date, but life on stone forts would have been very similar to life on a crannog. (Environment and Heritage Service, DOE(NI))

Pl 5: An Early Medieval multivallate ringfort on a drumlin hill at Lisleitrim, Co. Armagh overlooks a small lake within which there is a fine Early Medieval crannog. Crannogs could have functioned as permanent dwellings, summer lodges or even bolt-holes in the Early Medieval 'royal' settlement landscape. (Environment and Heritage Service, DOE (NI))

Pl 6: A crannog on Lough Meelagh, Co. Roscommon illustrates how many of these sites would have been fairly inaccessible except by boat, suggesting that some could have been used for refuge and defence. (Chris Corlett)

Pl 7: A small crannog on Lough More, Bofeenaun, Co. Mayo, recently dated to the early ninth century AD. Archaeological excavations by the Irish Archaeological Wetland Unit on this isolated site indicate that it may have been mostly used for iron-working. (Irish Archaeological Wetland Unit, UCD)

Pl 8: A crannog at Rosses Point, Co. Sligo, with a stone causeway zigzagging out to it. Stone and timber causeways were often used to restrict access to these lake-dwellings, making them easier to defend against people unfamiliar with the twists and turns of the routeway. (Victor Buckley)

20

Pl 9: Recent archaeological excavations by John Bradley at Moynagh Lough crannog, Co. Meath have revealed important evidence for a multi-period lake dwelling, occupied from the Mesolithic to the ninth century AD. The Early Medieval crannog was enclosed within various types of wooden palisades during the eighth and ninth centuries AD, constructed of both roundwood and cleft oak timber. (John Bradley)

Pl 10: Underwater photograph of a well-preserved oak roundwood post in the murky waters off Goose Island, Lough Ennell, Co. Westmeath. This palisade has been dated to the late ninth to early tenth centuries AD. (Crannog Archaeological Project)

Pl 11: Post-and-wattle panels and brushwood spectacularly preserved in the rich, organic deposits of the Early Medieval crannog at Moynagh Lough, Co. Meath. These structures have provided much interesting information on the character and exploitation of woodlands in the period. (John Bradley)

Pl 12: A crannog on Lough Digh, Co. Fermanagh, with its timber revetments and palisades poking up out of the water. Dendrochronological or tree-ring dating studies have indicated that crannogs first start to be constructed in Ireland over an 80 year period in the late sixth and early seventh centuries AD. (Claire Foley)

Pl 13: The well-known crannog reconstruction built in the 1970s at Craggaunowen, Co. Clare. Its houses, post-and-wattle palisade and size give a reasonably good impression of what some of these lake-dwellings may have looked like in the Early Medieval and Late Medieval period. (Shannon Heritage and Banquets)

Pl 14: Modern crannog reconstruction at Ulster History Park, near Omagh, Co. Tyrone. It is likely crannogs would have been occupied through the winter, although no doubt structural repair would have been necessary after storms and wave damage. (Ulster History Park)

23

Pl 15: Modern reconstruction of a crannog at National Heritage Park, Ferrycarrig, Co. Wexford, based on the excavated archaeological evidence from Moynagh Lough, Co. Meath. Animal bone, food waste and other rubbish was often thrown outside the crannog palisade. These 'middens' provide vital information on early diet and economy. (National Heritage Park, Ferrycarrig, Co. Wexford)

Pl 16: Reconstruction of an Early Medieval roundhouse at National Heritage Park, Ferrycarrig, Co. Wexford, based on excavated evidence from Moynagh Lough crannog. The post-and-wattle walls and thatched roof give a good indication of the appearance of these houses, which would have been used for sleeping, cooking and some crafts. (National Heritage Park, Ferrycarrig, Co. Wexford)

Pl 17: Early Medieval ploughshares from Crannog 61, Rathtinaun, Co. Sligo, a site excavated by Joseph Raftery in the 1950s. Plough irons have occasionally been found on crannogs, possibly signifying that valuable farming equipment was kept on islands for protection. (Barry Raftery, UCD)

Pl 18: Rotary quernstone fragments on a crannog on Tully Lough, Co. Roscommon. These quern-stones were used for grinding corn and indicate the domestic nature of occupation on this site in the past. (Aidan O'Sullivan)

25

Pl 19: Early Medieval woodworking axes from Lough Gara, Co. Sligo, gathered by Joseph Raftery and other archaeologists during the 1950s when lake levels were artificially dropped. Woodworking tools, including axes, chisels, gouges and adzes are frequent finds on Irish crannogs, as the palisades, houses and other structures would have needed constant repair. (Barry Raftery, UCD)

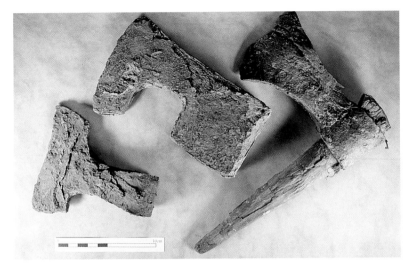

Pl 20: A tenth-century gaming board decorated in Scandinavian art style found on Ballinderry crannog No. 1, Co. Westmeath. This and several other finds from the site suggest that its inhabitants had close cultural, political and economic contacts with Viking Dublin. (National Museum of Ireland)

Pl 21: Early Medieval iron ladle from Crannog 61, Rathtinaun, Co. Sligo, possibly used for glass working or other industry. Some crannogs may have served as high-status craft centres patronised by kings and used by them as locations for the redistribution of goods through the wider social and economic landscape. (Barry Raftery, UCD)

0   10cm

Pl 22: Bone trial piece from Lagore crannog, Co. Meath. There is a range of evidence for bronze and glass working from Irish crannogs, and bone objects like this would have been used for working out designs before their application on metal. (National Museum of Ireland)

27

Pl 23: Belt-buckle of seventh to eighth century AD date from Lagore, Co. Meath. Brooches, pins, buckles and other high-status items of personal adornment have been found on several crannogs. (National Museum of Ireland)

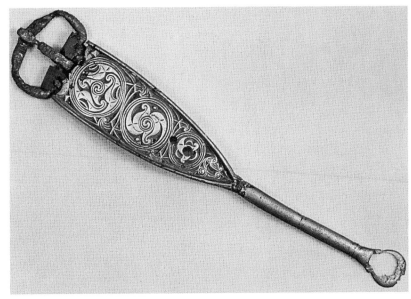

Pl 24: Early Medieval bone combs from various phases of occupation on Crannog 61, Rathtinaun, Co. Sligo. Bone, leather and woodworking, the manufacture of textiles and other crafts were all practised on crannogs, as they were at other secular and ecclesiastical settlements. (Barry Raftery, UCD)

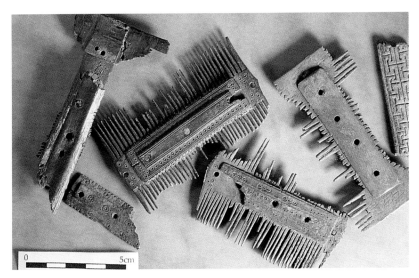

28

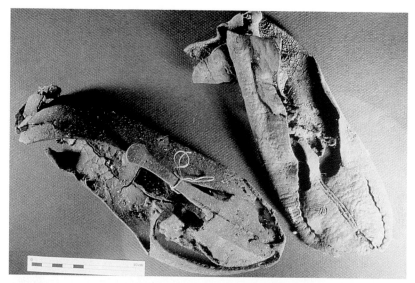

Pl 25: Early Medieval leather shoes from Crannog 61, Lough Gara, Co. Sligo. (Barry Raftery, UCD)

Pl 26: Two tiny glass vessels of seventh century date imported into Ireland from northern Europe, Moynagh Lough Crannog, Co. Meath. Imported pottery, glass and metalwork occasionally occur on Irish crannogs, indicating the far flung trading contacts between Early Medieval Ireland and Europe. (National Museum of Ireland)

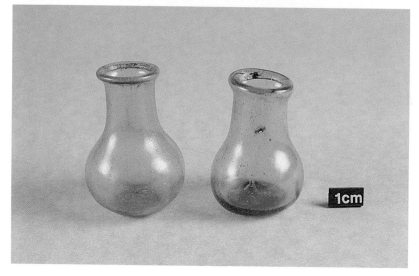

Pl 27: An eighth century bookshrine found underwater beside a crannog on Lough Kinale, Co. Longford. Crannogs may have been used as safe places to keep ecclesiastical metalwork during the turbulent years of the early ninth century, when both Irish and Viking armies were raiding monasteries and churches. (National Museum of Ireland)

Pl 28: A ninth to tenth century bronze ecclesiastical hand-bell found in water off a stone cairn crannog known as Castle Island, Lough Lene, Co. Westmeath. This object may also have been stored on the island for safekeeping. (National Museum of Ireland)

30

Pl 29: Eighth to ninth century copper-alloy wine strainer found on Moylarg crannog, Co. Antrim. Although this may well have been an ecclesiastical item, it could also have been used by the wealthy secular inhabitants of the site. (National Museum of Ireland)

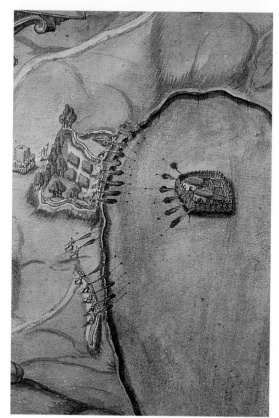

Pl 30: Detail of Richard Bartlett's pictorial map of an Irish crannog under attack by English forces in 1602. Crannogs were used in the 16th and 17th centuries by the Gaelic lords as places to store gold, silver, ammunition, or as dwellings for troops, prisoners and wounded. Their destruction during the Nine Years' War largely brought the tradition of crannog dwelling to an end. (National Library of Ireland)

Pl 31: 'Crannog ware' from Ballydoolough crannog, Co. Fermanagh. This type of crude, native pottery used for cooking is often found on crannogs in north-west Ireland and is an indicator of occupation on these sites in the Late Medieval period. (National Museum of Ireland)

Pl 32: Crannogs were not only defended strongholds for times of war, they were also lordly residences and summer lodges in times of peace. Richard Bartlett also illustrated crannogs in this map of Monaghan town, using folds in the map to symbolise the transition from the earlier Gaelic rural landscape to the new English planter town. (National Library of Ireland)

It is impossible to recognise any definite house structures amongst the thousands of vertical posts scattered across Lagore crannog, but it is certain that similar large dwellings would have been present on this important royal site.

Certainly, Irish crannogs had houses on them in the early seventeenth century. These small, thatched, rectangular or oval structures can be clearly seen in the maps of crannogs on Lough Roughan, County Tyrone, and on a lake in County Monaghan by the English cartographer Richard Bartlett. The archaeologist Richard Warner has suggested that some Irish Early Medieval crannogs could have been dominated by a single massive structure, whose side-walls consisted of the posts that we normally consider to be the site palisade.

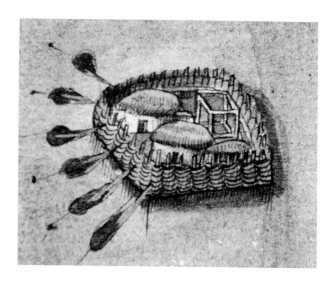

Fig. 14: Detail of Richard Bartlett's depiction of a crannog occupied in 1602. The pictorial map clearly shows that the crannog dwellers were living in small thatched houses, surrounded by a post-and-wattle palisade. Other enigmatic structures within the crannog remain to be explained. (National Library of Ireland)

Palisades

Palisades are usually interpreted either as a structural feature to prevent the cairn slumping outwards or as a defensive enclosing element. These wooden palisades vary in size and strength. At Craigywarren crannog, there is only a light enclosing palisade of widely spaced roundwood posts, with little sign of repair or reconstruction. At Lagore crannog, which was occupied over hundreds of years, it is obvious that there were several consecutive palisades of piles, posts and planks.

Defended entrances through which pathways led into the internal dwellings are also known, for example at Ballinderry crannog No. 1 and Moynagh Lough. Some crannogs also have an outer palisade, consisting of a loosely spaced ring of posts several metres out from the site. This feature could have been intended as a breakwater to protect the island from wave erosion. It could also have been to impede any enemies attacking by boat (see Fig. 1).

33

Fig. 15: The Early Medieval site of Ballinderry crannog No. 2, Co. Offaly under excavation by the Harvard Archaeological Expedition in the 1930s. The site was enclosed within a substantial wooden palisade. (Proceedings of the Royal Irish Academy)

Access by boat or causeway

Crannogs could occasionally be approached by means of stone or timber causeways. These are often ingeniously constructed, weaving erratically out to the site, and these sudden turns would have baffled and endangered any strangers approaching the sites with violence in mind.

Where no causeway existed, the only access to a crannog would have been by boat. Consequently, several crannogs have wooden slipways where boats could have been drawn up, safe from the effects of wind and wave. Dug-out boats were found at Lagore and Ballinderry crannog No. 2 and many crannogs are known to have dug-out boats lying beside them.

LIFE ON CRANNOGS

Farming and domestic economy

Crannogs would have served as the dwelling places of men, women and children, and for most of them, daily life would have revolved around the hours of work spent in producing and preparing food and raising their families. The diet of the crannog dwellers would have been based on the milk, eggs, grain and meat produced on the farmland around the crannog. While deer, fish and wildfowl could have been trapped by the lake, and certain plant-foods, nuts and berries could have been gathered, these wild foods would have been only an occasional supplement to the daily diet.

Despite their apparent isolation in a waterlogged landscape, Irish crannogs would

34

have been surrounded by an intensively managed agricultural landscape of farmsteads, field-systems and route-ways dispersed through a largely open, cleared landscape. Cattle herding would have been of great social and economic importance in the surrounding fields: land values were measured in terms of cattle and the size of a herd was the measure of a farmer's status. Such livestock as chickens, sheep, pigs and goats would also have been kept, some of them perhaps herded by the children of the crannog.

Fig. 16: Detail of roundwood post palisade, dated to early ninth century AD, at the metalworking crannog of Bofeenaun, Lough More, Co. Mayo. (Irish Archaeological Wetland Unit)

Wooden buckets and bowls found on crannogs were probably used by women for milking cattle, and for making butter and cheese. Indeed, scientific analyses of the cattle bones from Lagore and Moynagh Lough indicate that such work was the chief agricultural activity that sustained the

Fig. 17: Aerial photograph of crannog at Clea Lakes, Co. Down. The crannog is the small tree-clad island in the centre of the view, lying in a lake amidst rolling drumlin hills. Even within this difficult terrain, the crannog is deliberately inaccessible. (Cambridge University Committee for Aerial Photography AOX–93)

35

Fig. 18:
A crannog at
Kilcorran, Co.
Monaghan.
Although safety
and self-defence
were important
aspects of
crannog siting, it
is also clear that
proximity to other
secular and
ecclesiastical
dwellings,
routeways and
good agricultural
land were also
significant
factors. Crannogs
need to be studied
in relation to
these wider
landscapes.
(Dúchas – the
Heritage Service)

crannog community. Dairy cows predominated in the herds: male calves were killed off at a young age and cows were only slaughtered when past their prime. Although it would have been impossible to house cattle within crannogs, they may have been sited at particular parts of lakes to control prime pasture on the neighbouring drylands. Byres and corrals on the lake-shore would have protected the herds from wild animals and raiding rivals.

It is worth remembering that the wealthier or more powerful inhabitants of crannogs might not themselves have farmed the surrounding land, but could have depended on client farmers to provide them with meat, dairy products, grain and other foodstuffs. The ancient laws of Ireland (the 'Brehon Laws') describe just such a relationship between kings, lords and their dependants. Indeed, the study of the agricultural economy of crannogs may have been skewed by our concentration on the royal crannogs of Lagore, Ballinderry crannogs No. 1 and No. 2 and Moynagh Lough, where the periodic 'royal' feasting may have totally biased the archaeological evidence in favour of high-status foods and delicacies.

While crannogs may have been deliberately built on sites adjacent to the best cattle grazing land, vegetable gardens and fields of arable crops could also have been cultivated at suitable locations. Plough irons, including both coulters and ploughshares, have been found at Lagore and Ballinderry crannog No. 1. Reaping

hooks or sickles have been found at Lagore, as well as billhooks. A wooden shovel is known from Moynagh Lough, while a possible iron spade-tip was found at Ballinderry crannog No. 2.

We also have actual physical evidence of crops, as a deposit of carbonised oats and barley was found at Lough Faughan crannog in County Down, suggesting that these foods were stored on the site and burnt by accidental fire. Wheat straw, possibly used for flooring, was found in a mass of organic debris at Lagore. Stone rotary querns (handmills for grinding corn), whole and fragmentary, are a common find on Irish crannogs and were no doubt used for making flour for the crannog inhabitants.

Craft and industry

It is likely that crannog-dwellers were largely self-sufficient in terms of domestic crafts. It is clear from the waterlogged remnants of wood found on many sites that alder, oak, yew, hazel and willow were all-important raw materials for woodworkers and carpenters. Crannogs typically produce a range of wooden artefacts, such as lathe-turned bowls, carved tubs, stave-built buckets, spoons and ladles and occasionally pieces of decorated wood.

Interestingly, a few crannogs, such as Lagore and Moynagh

Fig. 19: A dug-out boat excavated beside the multi-period Crannog 61, Rathtinaun, Co. Sligo. Many crannogs today have several wooden boats lying submerged in the water beside them, testifying to the importance of water-borne transport for crannog-dwellers. (Barry Raftery, UCD)

Fig. 20: A crannog at Gortinty Lough, Co. Leitrim. The organic-rich nature of these peaty islands and the fact that they are protected from browsing animals means that they are often heavily covered in trees and vegetation. (Chris Corlett)

37

Fig. 21:
Wooden ladles
and dippers
found at Lagore
crannog,
Co. Meath.
(Proceedings of
the Royal Irish
Academy)

Lough, have also produced some evidence for lathe-turning waste (the wooden 'cores' left after the bowls are complete). This suggests that wooden bowls may have been produced actually on-site, using easily assembled pole-lathes. Wooden bucket stave blanks were found at Moynagh Lough, suggesting that some coopering was being carried out there. Souterrain-ware pottery (from the sixth to the tenth centuries AD) and everted-rim ware pottery (from the fifteenth and sixteenth centuries AD) is also occasionally found on northern crannogs.

Bone-working and antler-working was also apparently a common craft on crannogs. Comb-makers in Early Medieval Irish society had low status, so finds indicating this perhaps suggest the range of social classes present at crannogs. Rathtinaun crannog in County Sligo, excavated in the 1950s by Joseph Raftery, produced a fine collection of bone combs and the large bone assemblages in crannog middens were probably treated as a ready supply of raw material.

We also know that textiles were produced on certain crannogs using wooden distaffs and spindles for spinning and looms for weaving. Fragments of fine textiles, wool and hair have been found on several crannog sites. A possible loom fragment was found at Lough Faughaun, while other weaving implements were found at Lagore.

Fig. 22: Pieces of
textile found on
Lagore crannog,
Co. Meath.
(Proceedings of
the Royal Irish
Academy)

38

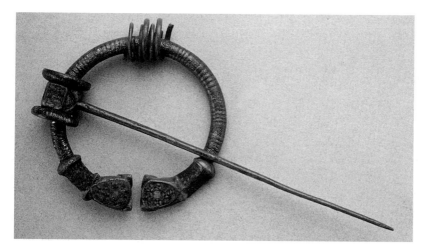

Fig. 23: Bronze zoomorphic pennanular brooch found on Ballinderry crannog No. 2, Co. Westmeath. Crannogs, like ringforts, often produce a range of high-status dress ornaments. (National Museum of Ireland)

Fig. 24: Bone motif piece from Moynagh Lough Crannog, Co. Meath. This site produced much evidence for on-site metalworking, including furnaces, copper ingots, crucibles as well as clay moulds. Bone motif pieces were used for working out and practising decorative designs. (John Bradley)

Leather working must have been practised on some sites as shoes, scraps of leather and a wooden shoe-last were found at Lagore, while iron tools for scoring leather are known from Lagore and Ballinderry crannog No. 1.

Some crannogs, like many ringforts and monastic sites, appear to have been places where small-scale copper and iron-working was carried out. Lagore and Moynagh Lough crannogs produced the clay crucibles used for melting copper and adding tin to make bronze artefacts. Mould fragments, in which brooches, rings, pins and other ornamented objects were cast, are also a familiar find from crannog sites,

39

Fig. 25: A modern re-enactor of Early Medieval warfare tactics and dress at the crannog reconstruction in the National Heritage Park, at Ferrycarrig, Co. Wexford. Swords, shield-bosses (the metal bowl-shaped front part of a wooden shield) and spearheads are frequently found on crannogs and are less common on other secular or ecclesiastical settlement sites. They indicate that soldiers and mercenaries would have been resident on many sites, while attacks on crannogs are also often mentioned in the early Irish annals. (National Heritage Park, Ferrycarrig, Co. Wexford)

and finds of 'motif pieces' show how their intricate designs were worked out by sketching or fine carving on discarded bones.

Crannogs were also used for small-scale iron working. Unprocessed iron ore, slag and iron bloom were found at Lough Faughaun crannog, iron slag was recovered from Ballinderry crannog No. 1 and iron furnace bottoms were found at Lagore. Indeed, an early ninth century crannog at Bofeenaun in County Mayo produced no evidence for occupation, but only iron slag and stone mortars, suggesting that it was a specialist site used in iron working. It may have been situated to exploit local bog or even mined ores as there is evidence of mines in the vicinity.

It is possible that some Early Medieval crannogs were important centres for fine metalworking and other specialist crafts. Indeed, the Scottish crannog expert Ian Morrison has suggested that Moynagh Lough could even be seen as a 'high-security island industrial estate' because of the range and quality of evidence found on that site. These crannogs may have acted as production centres and markets for the wider rural settlement and economic landscape.

Metalworkers, artisans and craftworkers resident on the crannog could have been under the protection and patronage of a local king. In exchange for the food and raw materials coming in to the crannog, there would have been high-quality goods and other artefacts going out of the lake-dwelling and into the surrounding landscape. Indeed, these items could have been distributed amongst the local communities as a means of recognising and strengthening the social and political ties between the king and the surrounding nobles and wealthy farmers.

Attack and defence

Crannogs would have been a good place to take refuge during the sudden, lightning raids that were typical of early Irish warfare, as the surrounding water and the wooden palisade would have discouraged any but the most determined of attackers. Early Medieval weaponry

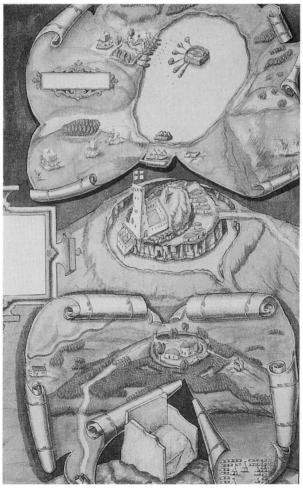

Fig. 26: A human skull covered in sword cut marks, found with an iron collar beside a crannog at Ardakillen, Co. Roscommon. These collars may have been used for holding hostages. (Wood-Martin's Lake Dwellings of Ireland, 1886)

Fig. 27: Richard Bartlett's depiction of an English attack upon a Gaelic Irish crannog in 1602. It is clear that the crannog served as a significant dwelling for the Gaelic Irish in the 16th and 17th centuries, although towerhouses and ringforts were as important. (National Library of Ireland)

41

(swords, spears, axes and the iron bosses of wooden shields) is commonly found on crannogs (in contrast to other settlement types) indicating the presence of warriors on these lake-dwellings.

There are also many Early Medieval and Late Medieval annalistic references to raids on crannogs, during which they were sacked, burned and abandoned. For example, we know from these sources that Lagore crannog, County Meath was attacked on several occasions between the seventh and tenth centuries AD. Early Medieval kings could also have used crannogs as bases for aggression against hostile neighbours.

The excavations at Lagore produced, apart from the unusually large number of weapons, a large amount of human bone derived from the decapitated corpses of men, women and children. Human bones, some with evidence for hacking or wounding, have also been found at Ballinderry crannog No. 1 in County Westmeath, Ardakillen crannog in County Roscommon and at Killyvilla Lake in County Monaghan. The incidence of human bones from crannogs which show such evidence for pre-mortem violence could also be taken as evidence for the execution of slaves or hostages and their ritual deposition as a gory sacrifice into the water.

Eamonn Kelly has suggested that crannogs may have been used as safe places to store ecclesiastical metalwork during the ninth century, when Viking raiders were marauding through the Irish midlands and north-west lakelands. This is because an eighth to ninth century book-shrine, a chalice and paten, a cross, as well as hand-bells have all been recovered from crannogs. For example, an eighth to ninth century book-shrine, chalice and paten were found near Lough Kinale crannog in County Longford, an eighth-century processional cross was found off a crannog in Tully Lough in County Roscommon, and ninth to tenth century bronze hand-bells have also been found near crannogs in Lough Ennell and Lough Lene.

Crannogs were used by Irish rebels against English rule in the early modern period. Muskets, armour, halberds, lead bullets and moulds for making bullets, all of sixteenth and seventeenth century date, have been found on several sites. Indeed, the various English military descriptions of failed assaults on crannogs during the Nine Years' War (1594–1603) indicate how difficult it must have been to attack these fortified lake-dwellings successfully.

Fig. 28: Reconstruction drawing of the large eighth century round house excavated by John Bradley at Moynagh Lough, Co. Meath. Its great size indicates that it was a 'royal' dwelling, used for feasting and assemblies. (John Bradley)

Crannogs and early Irish society

The settlement landscapes of early Ireland were organised in ways that reflect the highly stratified and hierarchical nature of their contemporary societies. It is unsurprising then that Early Medieval crannogs, like ringforts and monastic settlements, show evidence of having been occupied by a range of social classes.

The presence of slaves or hostages on some crannogs may be suspected from the discovery of iron collars with chains on Lagore crannog and beside Ardakillen crannog in County Roscommon. There might also have been various other unfree and free social classes present on a crannog, including the men and women who would have herded cattle, pigs and sheep, ploughed the land and re-built and repaired the crannog's palisades, pathways, houses and other structures. Carpenters, blacksmiths and other metalworkers, some of them of relatively high social status, might have occasionally been present on a lake-dwelling, while people proficient in lesser trades, such as weaving, bone-working and other crafts, may also have lived and worked on these islands.

43

Fig. 29: Aerial photograph of Lough Ennell, Co. Westmeath. The Early Medieval royal crannog of Cró-Inis can be seen out on the lake, with the royal ringfort of Dún na Sciath on the drylands nearby. A monastic site was located on Dysart Island beyond the crannog. Presumably, at certain times of the year, this lakeshore would have been a busy place, as craftsmen and women, soldiers, farmers and nobles congregated for the ceremonies associated with early Irish kingship. (Cambridge University Committee for Aerial Photography AVH–21)

It is also very likely that some Irish crannogs were the high-status residences of kings and their families, servants and retinue. Lagore, County Meath, Cró-Inis, County Westmeath and Island MacHugh, County Tyrone have all been historically identified as royal crannogs, while the dwellings and artefacts from Moynagh Lough suggest that it too was a royal site. The presence of exotic items on several other Irish crannogs (such as E-ware pottery from western France, Merovingian glass and

44

Frankish weaponry from northern Europe, silver from Hiberno-Norse Dublin and Anglo-Saxon England) testifies to the wealth and status of their royal inhabitants too.

A particularly important royal settlement complex is to be seen on the western shores of Lough Ennell, County Westmeath, where Dún na Sciath ringfort (the royal seat of Maélsechnaill, of the Clann Cholmáin kings of the southern Uí Neill dynasty) overlooks Cró-Inis crannog (the royal crannog). Probable royal crannogs and ringforts can be seen close together on several other lakes, such as at Lisleitrim, County Armagh, Levinallree, County Mayo and Coolure Demesne, County Westmeath.

It should also be possible to explore links between royal crannogs and that other important force in the Early Medieval Irish settlement landscape, the church. By the eighth century it was an important element in Irish society and it is not surprising that there is a range of evidence for contacts between crannog dwellers and local church authorities (for example, the ecclesiastical metalwork described above, the proximity of monastic enclosures to crannogs, and so on). It is obvious that the spatial and functional links between crannogs and ecclesiastical settlements would repay more research.

It is not clear as yet whether royal crannogs were permanent residences or temporary lodges, as mobility was an important aspect of early Irish kingship. The king may only have stayed on his crannog during his tour through the local territory, and could have gatherered his nobles and wealthy farmers around him for the occasional banquets associated with kingship. The large amounts of pig and cattle bone from crannog excavations at Lagore and Moynagh Lough may be evidence for such communal feasting. The king could also have stayed on his crannog when he was gathering horses and troops for a hosting.

However, while the king may have only been 'on-site' at certain times of the year, it is possible that the 'royal crannog' could have been the permanent dwelling of the king's retainers, herdsmen and artisans who would have maintained it through the winter storms.

SELECT BIBLIOGRAPHY

Bradley, J. 1991 Excavations at Moynagh Lough, County Meath. *Journal of the Royal Society of Antiquaries of Ireland* 111, 5–26

Fredengren, C. 1998 Lough Gara through time. *Archaeology Ireland* 12 (1), 31–3

Hencken, Hugh O'Neill, 1936 Ballinderry Crannog No 1. *Proceedings of the Royal Irish Academy* 43C, 103–239

Hencken, Hugh O'Neill, 1942 Ballinderry Crannog No 2. *Proceedings of the Royal Irish Academy* 47C, 1–76

Hencken, Hugh O'Neill, 1950 Lagore crannog: an Irish royal residence of the seventh to tenth century AD. *Proceedings of the Royal Irish Academy* 53C, 1–248

Johnson, R. 1999 Ballinderry Crannóg No 1: A reinterpretation. *Proceedings of the Royal Irish Academy* 99C, 23–71

Kelly, E.P. 1991 Observations on Irish lake-dwellings. In C. Karkov and R. Farrell (eds) *Studies in insular art and archaeology*, 81–98. American Early Medieval Studies 1. Cornell

Kelly, E.P. 1991 Crannogs. In M. Ryan (ed.) *The Illustrated archaeology of Ireland*, 120–3. Dublin

Morrison, I. 1985 *Landscape with lake dwellings: the crannogs of Scotland.* Edinburgh

O'Sullivan, A. 1998 *The archaeology of lake settlement in Ireland.* Discovery Programme Monographs 4, Discovery Programme/Royal Irish Academy, Dublin

O'Sullivan, A. 1998 Crannogs in contested landscapes. *Archaeology Ireland* 12 (2), 14–15

Warner, R. 1994 On crannogs and kings (Part 1). *Ulster Journal of Archaeology* 57, 61–9

Wood-Martin, W.G. 1886 *The lake-dwellings of Ireland.* Dublin

MODERN CRANNOG RECONSTRUCTIONS

National Heritage Park (Ferrycarrig)

Ferrycarrig, County Wexford

Tel. 053 20733

Opening times: April–November, daily 09.30–18.30

A large, well-made crannog reconstruction, based on the recently excavated 8th-century crannog levels at Moynagh Lough, County Meath, it has a palisade, boat quay and several large circular houses.

Craggaunowen

Kilmurray, Sixmilebridge, County Clare

Tel. 061 367178

Opening times: April – October, daily 10.00–6.00

The Craggaunowen crannog reconstruction is based on several excavated and surveyed sites and was built in the 1970s. It has an enclosing post-and-wattle palisade, a gang-plank, two circular houses and a gate tower.

Ulster History Park

Cullion, Lislap, Omagh, County Tyrone

Tel. 016626 48188

Opening times April–September 10.30–18.30

The Ulster History Park crannog has a post-and-wattle palisade, with internal structures consisting of both a circular and a rectangular house. There is also a gang-plank, the outline of another house, and a pole-lathe is set up within the site.

CRANNOGS

OTHER TITLES IN THE SERIES:

The Bend of the Boyne (Geraldine Stout, 1997)
***Early Celtic Art in Ireland** (Eamonn P Kelly, 1993)
***Early Irish Communion Vessels** (Michael Ryan, 2000)
Early Irish Monasteries (Conleth Manning, 1995)
Exploring the Burren (George Cunningham, 1998)
***The Fenians** (Michael Kenny, 1994)
Ireland's Archaeology from the Air (Tom Condit, 1997)
Irish Castles and Fortified Houses (David Sweetman, 1995)
Irish Dancing Costume (Martha Robb, 1998)
***Irish Furniture and Woodcraft** (John Teahan, 1994)
Irish High Crosses (Roger Stalley, 1996)
Irish Prehistory: An Introduction (Anna Brindley, 1995)
Irish Round Towers (Roger Stalley, 2000)
Irish Shrines and Reliquaries of the Middle Ages (Raghnall Ó Floinn, 1994)
Irish Wrecks of the Spanish Armada (Laurence Flanagan, 1995)
Megalithic Art in Ireland (Muiris O'Sullivan, John Scarey, 1993)
Metal Craftsmanship in Early Ireland (Michael Ryan, 1993)
***The Road to Freedom** (Michael Kenny, 1993)
***The 1798 Rebellion** (Michael Kenny, 1996)
***Sheela-na-Gigs** (Eamonn P Kelly, 1996)
Stone Circles in Ireland (Seán Ó Nualláin, 1995)
Walled Towns in Ireland (John Bradley, 1995)
Where Has Ireland Come From? (Frank Mitchell, 1994)

Published by Country House in association with the National Museum of Ireland

48